D1196094

TENNESSEE TITANS

BY TOM GLAVE

The Child's World®

Published by The Child's World®
1980 Lookout Drive • Mankato, MN 56003-1705
800-599-READ • www.childsworld.com

Acknowledgments
The Child's World®: Mary Berendes, Publishing Director
Red Line Editorial: Editorial direction
The Design Lab: Design
Amnet: Production

Design Element: Dean Bertoncelj/Shutterstock Images
Photographs ©: Charlie Riedel/AP Images, cover; Greg
McWilliams/Icon Sportswire, 5; Mark Humphrey/AP
Images, 7; Bettmann/Corbis, 9; Paul Spinelli/AP Images, 11;
Henryk Sadura / Shutterstock Images, 13; Doug Dukane/
AP Images, 14-15; Al Messerschmidt Archive/AP Images, 17;
Wesley Hitt/Icon Sportswire, 19; Wade Payne/AP Images,
21, 29; Peter Read Miller/AP Images, 23; Zach Bolinger/Icon
Sportswire, 25; Mark Zaleski/AP Images, 27

Copyright © 2016 by The Child's World®
All rights reserved. No part of this book may be
reproduced or utilized in any form or by any means
without written permission from the publisher.

ISBN 9781631439988
LCCN 2014959703

Printed in the United States of America
Mankato, MN
July, 2015
PA02265

ABOUT THE AUTHOR

Tom Glave grew up watching
football on TV and playing it
in the field next to his house.
He learned to write about
sports at the University of
Missouri-Columbia and has
written for newspapers in New
Jersey, Missouri, Arkansas, and
Texas. He lives near Houston,
Texas, and cannot wait to play
backyard football with his kids
Tommy, Lucas, and Allison.

TABLE OF CONTENTS

GO, TITANS!

The Titans quickly made a splash in Tennessee. They moved there from Houston in 1997. Tennessee had a magical 1999 season. The Titans moved into a new stadium in Nashville that year. They won all their home games. Tennessee made it all the way to the **Super Bowl**. The team has been a big hit ever since. Let's meet the Titans.

Defensive back Michael Griffin tackles Houston Texans quarterback Ryan Fitzpatrick in a game on October 26, 2014.

WHO ARE THE TITANS?

The Tennessee Titans play in the National Football **League** (NFL). They are one of the 32 teams in the NFL. The NFL includes the American Football Conference (AFC) and the National Football Conference (NFC). The winner of the AFC plays the winner of the NFC in the Super Bowl. The Titans play in the South Division of the AFC. They have played in one Super Bowl. They lost to the St. Louis Rams after the 1999 season.

Tennessee wide receiver Kevin Dyson comes up just short of the end zone on the final play of the Super Bowl on January 30, 2000.

WHERE THEY CAME FROM

The Titans **franchise** started in 1960 in Houston, Texas. The team was called the Oilers. They played in the American Football League (AFL). The Oilers won the first two AFL Championships. The league joined with the NFL after the 1969 season. So the Oilers did, too. Owner Bud Adams Jr. moved the team to Tennessee after the 1996 season. The team was called the Tennessee Oilers. Then they became the Titans in 1999.

Oilers running back Billy Cannon led the AFL with 948 rushing yards in 1961.

WHO THEY PLAY

The Tennessee Titans play 16 games each season. With so few games, each one is important. Every year, the Titans play two games against each of the other three teams in their division. They are the Indianapolis Colts, Jacksonville Jaguars, and Houston Texans. The Titans also play six other teams from the AFC and four from the NFC. The Titans played in the AFC Central before moving to the AFC South.

Titans defensive back Marqueston Huff sacks Jacksonville Jaguars quarterback Blake Bortles in a game on October 12, 2014.

WHERE THEY PLAY

The Titans have played in three stadiums since leaving Houston. They played in the Liberty Bowl in Memphis, Tennessee, in 1997. They played at Vanderbilt University in Nashville in 1998. The Titans moved to Adelphia Coliseum in Nashville in 1999. They won their first 12 games there. That is a record for a new stadium. The stadium is now called LP Field. It holds 69,143 fans. It also hosts college football games and concerts.

LP Field sits next to the Cumberland River, just a short walk from downtown Nashville.

THE FOOTBALL FIELD

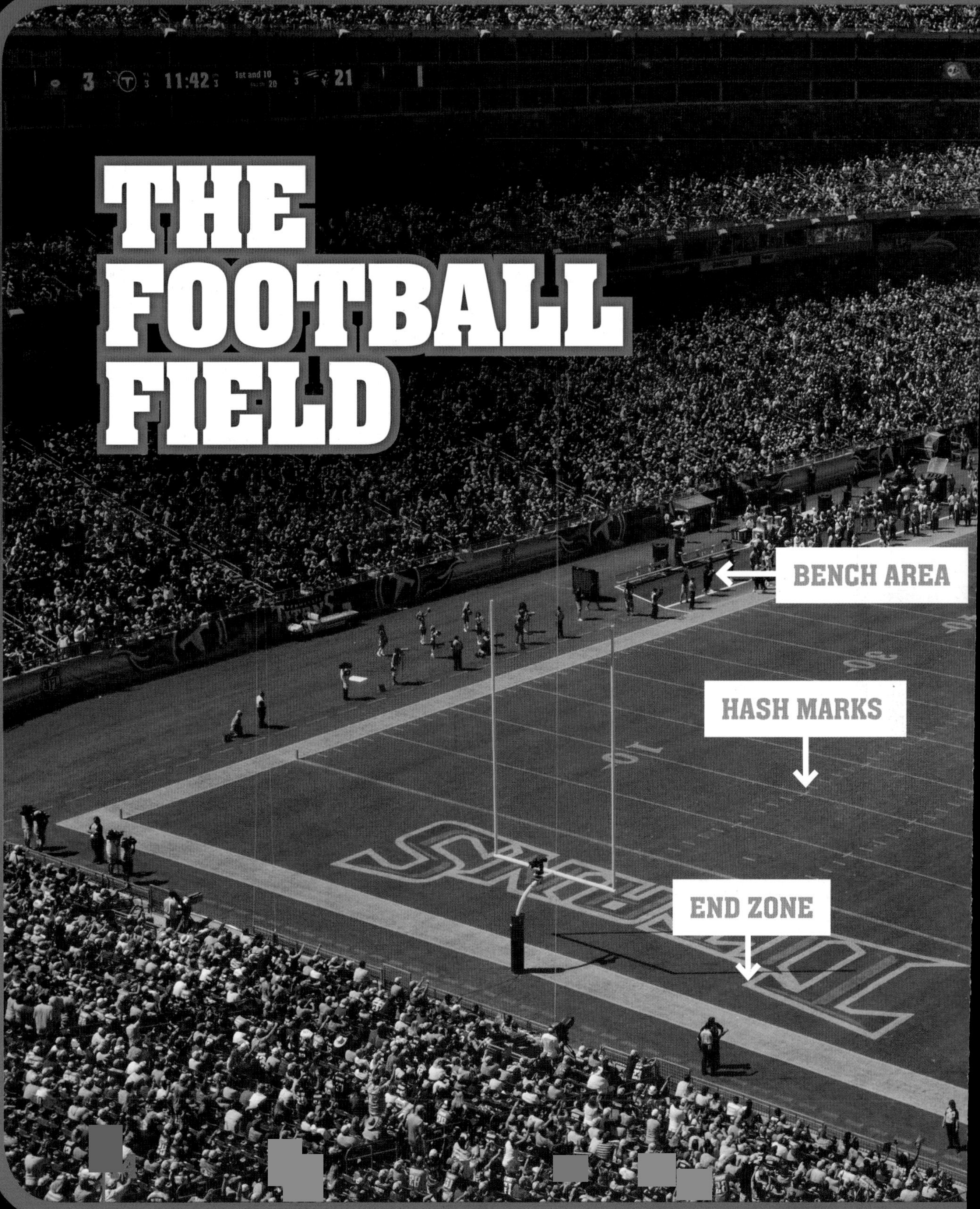

BENCH AREA

HASH MARKS

END ZONE

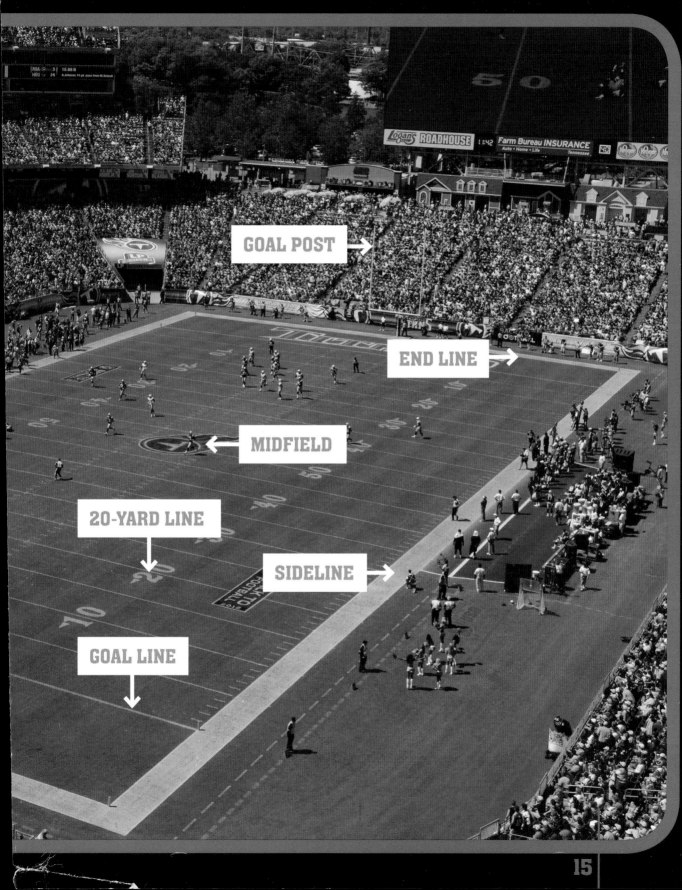

GOAL POST

END LINE

MIDFIELD

20-YARD LINE

SIDELINE

GOAL LINE

BIG DAYS

The Titans have had some great moments in their history. Here are three of the greatest:

1984—The Houston Oilers signed quarterback Warren Moon. He was a star in the Canadian Football League. He was also great in the NFL. Moon played with Houston from 1984 to 1993. He made six **Pro Bowls** in that time.

2000—The 1999 Titans' incredible Super Bowl run almost ended on January 8, 2000. Tennessee was losing to the Buffalo Bills in the **playoffs**. There were three seconds left. Tight end Frank Wycheck fielded a kickoff. He threw a **lateral** across the field. Wide receiver Kevin Dyson caught it. He ran up the sideline for a touchdown. Tennessee won 22-16. The game is called "The Music City Miracle."

Wide receiver Kevin Dyson (87) sprints down the sideline during "The Music City Miracle," one of the most incredible plays in NFL history.

2000—The Titans had won their first 11 games at Adelphia Coliseum. Then they beat the Pittsburgh Steelers 9-7 there on November 5. It was Tennessee's 12th straight home win. That set an NFL record for a new stadium.

TOUGH DAYS

Football is a hard game. Even the best teams have rough games and seasons. Here are some of the toughest times in Titans history:

1973—The Oilers ended the 1972 season with 11 straight losses. They then lost the first seven games of the 1973 season. It is the longest losing streak in franchise history through 2014.

1993—The 1992 Oilers made the playoffs. They played the Buffalo Bills on January 3. Houston led 35-3 in the second half. But Buffalo scored 35 straight points to take the lead. Houston tied the game 38-38 late in the fourth quarter. But the Oilers lost in **overtime**. It is the biggest comeback in NFL history through 2014.

Coach Jeff Fisher (right) left the Titans after the 2010 season.

2011—Jeff Fisher had been the team's only coach in Tennessee. He had led the Titans to their Super Bowl appearance. But after more than 16 seasons it was time for a change. He left the team on January 27.

MEET THE FANS

Fans in Nashville love the Titans. LP Field has been sold out for every home game. Nashville is famous for country music. It is known as "Music City." Game days showcase this. Fans enjoy concerts at the stadium. Popular musicians perform before the game and during stops in play. T-RAC also entertains fans. He is a raccoon mascot. Raccoons are the state animal of Tennessee. Sometimes, T-RAC dresses up with a helmet and sword.

Mascot T-RAC often dresses in different outfits to entertain fans during Titans home games.

HEROES THEN

The Titans franchise has had some great running backs. Earl Campbell led the NFL in rushing yards his **rookie** season. He was named NFL Rookie of the Year and Most Valuable Player in 1978. Eddie George rushed for more than 10,000 yards in his career. He started every game for Tennessee from 1996 to 2003. Chris Johnson ran for 2,006 yards in 2009. Only four players had rushed for more in a season. Quarterback Warren Moon was great. He led the Oilers to seven straight playoff appearances. Moon led the NFL in passing yards and touchdowns in 1990.

Quarterback Warren Moon entered the Pro Football Hall of Fame in 2006.

HEROES NOW

Wide receiver Kendall Wright was drafted in 2012. He led the Titans in receptions in his first two NFL seasons. No other Titan had done that. Wright also set a team record with 158 combined catches in 2012 and 2013. Defensive back Jason McCourty is a veteran leader. He had four interceptions in 2012. He also had a team-best 46 passes defended between 2011 and 2013.

Defensive back Jason McCourty (below) breaks up a pass in a game against the Indianapolis Colts on December 1, 2013.

GEARING UP

NFL players wear team uniforms. They wear helmets and pads to keep them safe. Cleats help them make quick moves and run fast. Some players wear extra gear for protection.

THE FOOTBALL

NFL footballs are made of leather. Under the leather is a lining that fills with air to give the ball its shape. The leather has bumps or "pebbles." These help players grip the ball. Laces help players control their throws. Footballs are also called "pigskins" because some of the first balls were made from pig bladders. Today they are made of leather from cows.

Wide receiver Kendall Wright has been an important part of the offense since Tennessee drafted him in 2012.

HELMET

SHOULDER PADS

GLOVES

THIGH PADS

FOOTBALL

CLEATS

SPORTS STATS

ere are some of the all-time career records for the Tennessee Titans. All the stats are through the 2014 season.

RECEPTIONS

Ernest Givins 542

Haywood Jeffires 515

RUSHING YARDS

Eddie George 10,009

Earl Campbell 8,574

INTERCEPTIONS

Jim Norton 45

Cris Dishman 31

TOTAL TOUCHDOWNS

Eddie George 74

Earl Campbell 73

SACKS

Ray Childress 75.5

William Fuller 59

POINTS

Al Del Greco 1,060

Rob Bironas 1,032

Quarterback Steve McNair made the Pro Bowl three times in his 11 seasons with the team.

PASSING YARDS

Warren Moon 33,685

Steve McNair 27,141

GLOSSARY

franchise a team that is part of a professional sports league

lateral when a player throws the ball backward or sideways

league an organization of sports teams that compete against each other

overtime extra time that is played when teams are tied at the end of four quarters

playoffs a series of games after the regular season that decides which two teams play in the Super Bowl

Pro Bowls the NFL's All-Star game, in which the best players in the league compete

rookie a player playing in his first season

Super Bowl the championship game of the NFL, played between the winners of the AFC and the NFC

FIND OUT MORE

IN THE LIBRARY

Gigliotti, Jim. *Super Bowl Super Teams.*
New York: Scholastic, 2010.

Gilbert, Sara. *The Story of the Tennessee Titans.*
Mankato, MN: Creative Education, 2014.

Stewart, Mark. *The Tennessee Titans.*
Chicago: Norwood House, 2013.

ON THE WEB

Visit our Web site for links about the Tennessee Titans:
childsworld.com/links

Note to Parents, Teachers, and Librarians: We routinely verify our Web links to make sure they are safe and active sites. So encourage your readers to check them out!

INDEX